LOCOMOTIVES
in detail

| RIDDLES CLASS 9F | 7 | 2-10-0 |

LOCOMOTIVES
in detail
7

RIDDLES CLASS 9F   **2-10-0**

DAVID CLARKE

Ian Allan
PUBLISHING

I am old enough to have seen many of the 9Fs in traffic and also under overhaul at Crewe works, but unfortunately I never managed to be on a train hauled by one. Even when they were in a filthy, unkempt state (which was most of the time) they had an air of muscular competence about them and always appeared in total control of whatever train being hauled. I remember watching No. 92167 easing away from a signal stop at Shrewsbury station with a heavy oil train in 1965 without the hint of any wheel slippage and in total control of the train. The 9Fs were never less than impressive.

The 9F from a detail point of view are deceptively complex with many of the detail changes being very subtle and not always easy to spot in photographs. The Engine History Cards have been analysed but, as with other classes the cards suffer from not being fully updated from 1964 onwards so many of the later changes (such as tenders) were not officially recorded. So to identify many of these latter changes I have used an extensive collection of photographs and observations from such as the *Railway Observer*. Where I have used previously published lists for changes and variants I have validated this with photographic evidence and where the photograph contradicts the published data I have not used the published sources. In the course of researching for this book I came across a number of contradictory statements, so if there are any errors they are mine not a simple reiteration of 'facts' from an unknown source.

The class has been extensively covered in book form so the obvious question to ask is 'what does this book have to offer' beyond the obvious one of having colour photographs? I have tried to summarise all the detailed changes in a compact format so that when viewing a photograph the reader should be able to identify any changes made to that particular locomotive. The objective of this series is to show the detail variations within the class in an easily understandable form and where possible, tables have been used to summarise the as-built configuration and allow easy reference, while the text describes subsequent changes. The photographs have been chosen to show as many of the possible variations through the class. I have managed to identify one small variation that I have not seen recorded elsewhere. Some of the Western Region locomotives had a long rectangular-shaped plate fitted over the reverser shaft presumably as a safety measure to provide a sound foothold for crews working on the platform.

Producing a book is not a solitary process; and a number of people have provided help and assistance in me producing this book.

Thanks to Ron White at Colour Rail for digging through his archive of colour photographs for items not used before and to John Jennison for his help and in checking the text. Pat Jarvis formerly a fireman at Annesley gave me some insights into the class when working from that depot. Brian Stickland and Don McNab both of whom are part of the group who have restored No. 92214 for both help and advice. Also for some cab photos of their locomotive. There are also a number of excellent web sites the best two being those run by the group owning Nos. 92214 and 92219 is *www.92214.co.uk* and the site for the group owning No. 92212 is *www.92212.com*.

Ironically the office, in which I am based (north of Nottingham) for my day job, is built on the site of Annesley yard and shed, the home of so many 9Fs. So if I close my eyes I can almost hear the ghostly sounds of the trains leaving the yard with the famous 'windcutter' trains.

David Clarke, Derby, March 2007

Recommended reading:
BR Standard Steam Locomotives Volume 1. RCTS. This volume covers the background to the building of the standard classes.
The Book of the 9Fs. Irwell Press 2006. Again excellent photographic coverage and detailed captions. Recommended.
The BR Standard 9F 2-10-0. Philip Atkins. Irwell Press 1993. An excellent book covering much of the background to the design. Now out of print.
The Power of the 9Fs. Gavin Morrison. Oxford Publishing. 2001. A good photographic study.
Locomotive Profile No 33. Brian Reed. 1973. An excellent summary of the class. Now long out of print.
British Railway Standard Steam Locomotives. Ted Talbot, Oxford Publishing 1982. A good photographic review of all the standard classes.
Locomotive Panorama Volume 1. E. S. Cox. Ian Allan 1966. This gives an authoritative insight into the development and production of the standard classes from someone who was intimately involved in the process and decision making. Strongly recommended.
A number of excellent articles by David Percival on the use of the 9Fs on passenger services were published in three issues of *Steam World* (September, October and November 2002) and are thoroughly recommended and worth finding secondhand copies.

Series Created & Edited by Jasper Spencer-Smith.
Design and artwork: Nigel Pell.
Produced by JSS Publishing Limited, P.O. Box 6031, Bournemouth, Dorset, England.
Colour Scanning: JPS Ltd, Branksome, Poole, Dorset, BH12 1DJ.

First published 2007

ISBN (10) 0 7110 *3246 7*
ISBN (13) 978 0 7110 *3246 0*

Published by Ian Allan Publishing

an imprint of Ian Allan Publishing Ltd, Hersham, Surrey KT12 4RG.
Printed in England by Ian Allan Printing Ltd, Hersham, Surrey KT12 4RG.

Code: 0706/B2

Visit the Ian Allan Publishing website at www.ianallanpublishing.com

Title spread: No. 92220 *Evening Star* heads the 'Capitals United Express' between London and South Wales in July 1960 (see page 57) when allocated to Cardiff (Canton). (CR)

Photograph Credits
Colour-Rail (CR) and their photographers
M. Chapman (MC); Derek Cross (DC); P.A. Fry (PAF);
Tommy Tomalin (TOM); C. R. Gordon Stuart (CGS);
G. Warnes (GW).
Ian Allan Library (IA)
J.R. Carter (JRC); G.P. Cooper (GPC); J. Davenport (JD);
M. Dunnett (MD); Ian G. Holt (IGH); M. Mensing (MM);
N.E. Preedy (NEP); Paul Riley (PR); R.E. Ruffell (REF);
P.J. Sharpe (PJS); C. Sheard (CS); David Smith (DS);
Verdun Wake (VW); Rodney Wildsmith (RW); N.R. Wood (NRW).
Others;
Authors Collection (AC),
John Jennison (JJ),
Michael Mensing (MM).

INTRODUCTION

The objective was to design a range of standard
locomotives that could run on any of the regions
and incorporate best practice from all sources.

With the formation of British Railways on 1 January 1948 a new strategy was required for the forward direction of motive power and the issue could be distilled into two options:

1 Allow the newly formed Regions (based very much on the former 'Big Four' companies) to continue to design and build their own designs, independently of the other regions.

2 Develop a range of 'Standard' locomotives that could run on any of the regions and incorporate best practice, not only from within the UK but from the rest of the world, particularly from the USA. This standard range would be the only new build allowed until electrification could commence.

It became clear almost immediately that the preferred option would be to design a range of standard steam locomotives and to stop building any of the former railway company designs. One of the principal reasons behind this decision was to reduce both the cost of building and the operating costs. In the postwar period there was recognition that there would be labour shortages in the area of locomotive maintenance and that any new designs should incorporate these principles.

However, it would take time to design and build these new locomotives and for a short period some existing designs continued to be built to fill the gap before the standard classes became available. Examples of former 'Big Four' classes built in this way include, LNER A1 4-6-2 (21 built), LNER A2 4-6-2 (14 built), ex-LMS Black 5 (40 built), GWR Castle (30 built).

A total of 1,538 locomotives of 'Big Four' designs were built after the formation of British Railways (BR) and before any of the BR 'Standard' classes were introduced.

As a precursor to the production of any standard designs and to assist in the design process, locomotive trials were arranged in 1948 where the most modern locomotives in a number of categories were run on other regions and comparisons made on some key criteria, such as average and maximum power also coal consumption.

The list of standard locomotives had four completely new designs (the 'Britannia', 'Clan', 'Duke of Gloucester' and the 9F), four new designs based on existing types and four using existing designs with only minor modifications. The decision on which design to proceed with first was driven by operating considerations, the most pressing need was for a Class 7 to improve services on the Great Eastern section of the Eastern Region, so the 'Britannia' became the first 'Standard' class locomotive to enter service.

Above:
No. 92227 at Banbury, September 1965 in typical 9F condition. Built from new with a double chimney, the BR1G tender is retained from service on the WR where it worked until October that year. No. 92227 was then moved to Warrington and subsequently Speke Junction. (AC)

Left: No. 92088 in ex-works condition at Weedon (Northampton), October 1961. The locomotive was initially allocated to the Eastern Region hence the BR1F tender, but was allocated to the London Midland Region, when moved from Annesley to Leicester in February 1963. (CR/TOM)

No. 92243 at Banbury, July 1966, fitted with a BR1G tender and the Western Region route availability 'spot' under the number. The 9F in the shed has Birkenhead stencilled on the buffer beam and carries a replacement wooden smoke box door number plate. (IA)

There are many who questioned the wisdom of designing a new range of locomotives rather than continue to build designs from the former companies but this does not form the *raison d'etre* of this book, my role is to detail what was built not to challenge why.

WHY A 2-10-0?

Before considering the design in detail we need to consider why the 2-10-0 arrangement was agreed to as this was not a common wheel arrangement on the British network. Heavy freight locomotives in the UK were usually 2-8-0s. One of the design principles was that the new heavy freight locomotive should be capable of hauling heavy freight trains at higher speed than had been previously been the norm. The mineral train schedules in use called for an average speed of 17 to 25mph (27 to 40kph) with a maximum of 40mph (64.4kph). BR was now looking for average speeds of 35mph (56kph) with a maximum of 50mph (80.5kph). This set the design team a problem as the narrow firebox-type boilers of conventional 2-8-0 designs (such as the Stanier 8F, GWR 36 and 47xx and LNER O4) would not be able to supply sufficient steam. Therefore the proposals focussed on two alternative approaches, a 2-8-2

Right:
Nos. 92153 and 92156 at Bedford on the Midland mainline on a test train in March 1959. Tests with 9Fs had first been run on the Midland in February 1955 to determine loadings between the Nottingham coal fields and London. Further tests in 1958 used the LMS dynamometer car on tests between Toton Yard (between Derby and Nottingham) and Brent in north London. (AC)

Above:
No. 92123 at Bulwell (near Nottingham) on the ex-GCR mainline in June 1965. The locomotive was allocated to Birkenhead. The tender is a BR1C fitted from new. (AC)

and a 2-10-0. The design of the new heavy freight locomotive was left until many of the other standard classes had been designed, so that by mid-1950 the final outline arrangement for the class had still not been agreed as the design team's efforts had been focussed on the 'Britannia' and the mixed traffic classes. As the 9F was left until last it had been hoped to utilise some of the major components from some of the other standard classes so an early proposal included using the boiler of the 'Clan' on a 2-8-2 chassis and subsequent proposals included using the boiler from the 'Britannia', again as a 2-8-2.

In 1950 E.S. Cox (a senior member of the design team) put forward a comparison between a 2-8-2 and 2-10-0 with a recommendation that the 2-8-2 be the preferred design. In line with the consideration of design practices in other countries, the 2-8-2 had proved to be very popular in the USA with many thousands of locomotives built to this successful design. However Riddles (who headed the design team) had a preference for the 2-10-0 (having been responsible for the design of the wartime WD 2-10-0s, of which 150 were built) and further consideration was given on solving the

major problem of the 2-10-0 design, how to get a wide firebox boiler of adequate proportions above 5ft (1.5m) driving wheels (the WD had 4ft 8in [1.4m] driving wheels), have space for a decent sized ash pan and also ensure good airflow into the firebox. In June 1951 one of the design team (G. G. Carrier) produced a diagram which showed details of an ash pan design that satisfied all the design criteria and enabled a satisfactory 2-10-0 design to be undertaken. Therefore in July 1951 approval was given to the 2-10-0 configuration and detailed design could commence.

The debate within the Railway Executive between R.A. 'Robin' Riddles, his assistant Roland Bond and E.S. Cox had been vigorous with both Bond and Cox in favour of the 2-8-2 proposal but in the end it was Riddles who made the final decision. Following his retirement, Bond, in his memoirs written 25 years later, was still insisting that if the decision had been his he would have gone with the 2-8-2 proposal!

We shall never know which design was the better, but certainly the final version of 2-10-0 proved to be one of the most successful locomotive designs ever produced and operated on the British network.

92024

CHAPTER ONE

DESIGN

The BR 9F proved to be one of the most successful designs
ever produced and operated on the British railway network.

n 1948, the newly formed British Railways
(BR) set up a design team under Riddles to
design and build a range of 'Standard' steam
locomotives to fill the gap before the railway
network was electrified. The design of the BR
'Standards' was intended to take the best practice
not only from the previous companies but also
from foreign practice. During World War Two
some of the features of the US-built S160 class
2-8-0 locomotive attracted some attention as
390 of these were operating on the British
network (all were shipped to continental Europe
following the invasion) enabling the S160 to be
studied in close detail. These locomotives had
wide fireboxes over the rear trailing axle, a high
running plate and incorporated the use of rocker-
type ash grate and self-cleaning smoke box to
make ash/clinker disposal easier and quicker.
These US-built locomotives considerably
influenced the design of the 'Austerity' class
2-8-0 and 2-10-0 (particularly the latter) with
the use of a wide firebox over the driving wheels,
down to the very neat austere-shaped chimney.
The design of the WD 2-10-0 influenced
Riddles of the merits of the type and convinced
him to go with this configuration when
sketching out the basic layout for 9Fs.
In addition to having a US-built locomotive to
study at close quarters; a number of senior
engineers from LMS and LNER visited the

USA at the end of the war to study railway
practice. The group visited nine US railroad
companies to gather information.

Also some of the principal members of the
BR design team also travelled abroad and had
been influenced by what they had seen.
The LMS led the way after the war with H. A.
Ivatt incorporating self-cleaning smoke boxes,
rocker-type ash grates, manganese-bronze
bearings and roller bearings in the last LMS
designs. Many of these features were to be
incorporated into the new BR 'Standard'
designs, also best engineering practice from the
pre-nationalised companies was also considered.
Each design in the range was allocated a drawing
office which took prime responsibility for the
design, but had to use components from a
standard list. These components were designed at
various works. For instance, Derby was
responsible for the design of the tenders, wheels,
axles and springs with Doncaster being
responsible for cylinders and valve gear.

The Brighton drawing office had overall
responsibility for the complete design of the 9F
under the supervision of R. G. Jarvis (who was also
responsible for the rebuilding of the 'Merchant
Navy' and 'West Country' class 4-6-2 Pacifics).
A number of early proposals such as the use of
roller bearings, the multiple valve regulator (both
used on the 'Britannia') and cast frames were

The firebox side and cab front showing the steam manifold connected (via the rectangular cover) to the exhaust ejector. The reverser shaft can be seen on the top of the footplate.
A flat cover plate was fitted to a small number of WR locomotives, presumably to provide a better foothold when walking on the platform. (AC)

9

abandoned. The design team was able to take into account the operating experience gained from the 'Standard' classes already in service. So for example the problems with the 'Britannia'-type fluted coupling rod led to a redesigned plain section rod being incorporated into the 9F. The design was based on the rods used on the WD 2-10-0. To aid the Doncaster team a WD 2-10-0 was temporarily allocated to Doncaster shed for a short period (the WD 2-10-0s were all allocated to Scottish depots).

The key features of the 9Fs were as follows:
1 The horn guides for the axle boxes were located in the centre of the frames making the frames closer together, this had been developed by Bullied for the 'Merchant Navy' class and the intention here was to produce a set of rigid frames resistant to cracking. This design had been used successfully on the 'Britannia' and when applied to the 9F produced strong and trouble free frames and an excellent ride. This was one of the contributing factors which allowed drivers to push the locomotive to high operating speeds.

2 The use of a wide firebox on a freight locomotive. Whilst this boiler configuration was not unusual in Europe or in the USA it was unusual in the UK, the only previous use had been on the WD 2-10-0s produced during the World War Two.
3 The use of 10 driving wheels for a freight locomotive, this again followed the WD version in being fitted with flangeless centre driver wheels.
4 Reciprocating balance (omitted from the WD locomotives) was set at 40% and following experimental work at Brighton on cross balancing, saved a considerable amount of lead weight on the main driving wheels thus reducing hammer blow. The riding qualities of the class were excellent, enabling the 9F to run comfortably at speeds well in excess of the 60mph (96.6kph) maximum of the design brief.
5 The cab and foot plating was suspended from the boiler (not on the frames) in the same way as on the 'Britannia' but unlike that class, the cab floor was extended but not over to the front of the tender.

Above: The US-built S160 class 2-8-0s were used on UK railways during the 1940s before being shipped to Europe. Many features on these locomotives influenced the designers of the LMS and BR Standard classes. (IA)

Left: No. 90773, a WD 2-10-0 at South Leith, August 1962. This class of locomotive was designed by R. A. Riddles during World War Two, and heavily influenced the design of the 9F. (IA)

Right: The cab back head on No. 92214 showing, at centre, the two water level gauges. The green fixture on the left is the warning bell which is part of the ATC system. (AC)

Right: The left-hand side of the cab with the driver's seat just visible. The red wheel is the reverser which on the 9F was at 90⁰ to the position of most other steam locomotives. It was nicknamed the 'mangle', alluding to the handwashing mangle in the days before washing machines. The cylinder cut-off percentage numbers can be seen to the left of the wheel. (AC)

A conventional fall plate was fitted to the tender.

6   Steeply inclined cylinders. This allowed the largest possible cylinders to be used within the loading gauge. A similar arrangement was used on the ex-LMS 'Crab' 2-6-0 to provide clearance for the large cylinders. The cylinders and piston valves on the 9F were the same as those fitted to the 'Britannia' class, being 20in (50.8cm) bore and 28in (71cm) stroke.

7   The necessity of pitching the boiler as high as possible (to allow an adequate ash pan) meant that the proposal to use the 'Britannia'-type boiler had to be abandoned and a new design produced. However some of the flanging blocks from the 'Britannia' class were used.

8   The use of smoke deflectors on a freight locomotive. Up until the introduction of the 9F only express passenger locomotives had previously been so fitted. It was unusual for a freight locomotive to have them from new and before any service on passenger trains would have justified fitment.

Much thought went into the design of the cab and operating controls with a full-size mock up being constructed for assessment by driving staff and comment from operational crews. One major change was that the reversing wheel was placed at 90^0 to the conventional position.

The 9F boiler was one of four new wide firebox-type boilers designed for the new 'Standard' classes (the other three being the 'Clan', 'Duke of Gloucester' and the 'Britannia') the other 'Standards' classes utilising boilers based on existing companies designs (such as the BR 'Standard' class 5 utilising a boiler essentially the same as that on the LMS class 5.).

Following post-war Southern Railway and LMS practice the firebox was fitted with a rocking grate which enabled the fireman to break up clinker and allow ash to fall into the ash pan whilst the engine was in motion. The ash pans were fitted with bottom doors (following post-war LMS practice) enabling the ash pan to be emptied by using an external lever. This made ash disposal much easier (and safer as the yard staff did not need to use fire irons when raking out clinker).

Above: No. 92214 at Barrow Hill shed showing the exhaust ejector to the right of the smoke deflector and the clack valves on the side of the boiler. (AC)

Right: No. 92203 showing the associated pipe work for the two injectors, one exhaust (with the larger pipe) and the live steam (the outside one of the pair). (AC)

Left: The designers of the 9F mounted the largest cylinder that would fit within the British loading gauge. These cylinders were the same size as used on the 'Britannia' 20in (50.8cm) diameter and 28in (71cm) stroke. The crosshead and slide bar design followed LNER practice. (AC)

Unusually for a freight locomotive many were fitted with double blast pipe and double chimney. This resulted from the scientific approach to blast pipe design being carried out at Swindon Works by S. O. Ell.

The wheels were of standard construction with the balancing weights formed by steel plates sandwiching the spokes and riveted through from front to back following LMS practice.

A total of five different tender types were coupled to 9F class locomotives with various combinations of coal and water capacity to suit the requirements of the regions where the locomotives were initially allocated.

Left: The space between the top of the frames and the underside of the boiler is clearly shown as is the feed pipe (on the far side) for the sand boxes (the fillers were only on the fireman's side). The middle driving wheel is flangeless. Because the axle boxes are centred in the frames there is a noticeable gap between the back of the wheels and the frames. (AC)

Right: The two doors to facilitate the raking out of the ash pan are shown here in the closed position. Most 9Fs ran with the doors in the open position. The battery box for the ATC is under the cab and the associated conduit runs under the bottom edge of the platform. The bar protruding from behind the rear driving wheel is for operating the rocker grate. (AC)

Right: The substantial brackets required to attach the two injectors (exhaust and live steam) on the fireman's side of the cab are visible on this unrestored 9F. (AC)

Left: The dual purpose bracket that supports the slide bars and for mounting the lubricator are clearly visible. The brackets attached to the boiler for supporting the platform can also be seen as well as the large bracket supporting the boiler. (AC)

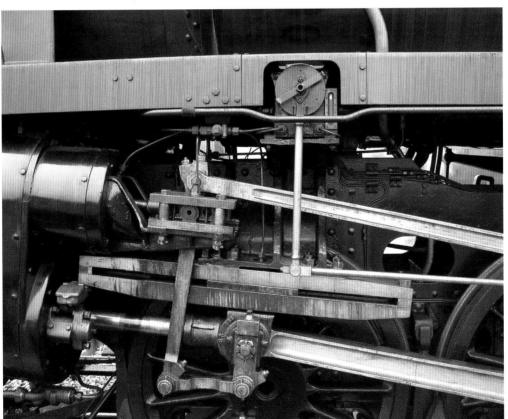

Left: The crosshead and piston valves and the associated drive mechanism to drive the lubricator when in motion. When first built the access hole in the platform valance was smaller and revised to what is shown. The conduit under the valance is part of the ATC fitment. (AC)

No. 92205 after service on the SR (Eastleigh and Feltham) with the additional lamp brackets either side of the smokebox door handle. The locomotive is at Carlisle with a limestone train to Ravenscraig steelworks at Motherwell, Scotland, August 1964. The locomotive shows WR origins with a BR1G tender and ATC equipment. The original steps below the smokebox are retained. (IA/DS)

The motion and driving wheel showing the substantial connecting rods. The eccentric has the modified LMS-style four bolt fixing (replacing the original LNER-type fitment). The wheels have a completely flat face and the axle has a hole bored through. (AC)

9 F

2214

The entrance to the cab. The battery box for the ATC can be seen below the cab side. The pipe below the battery box and to the right of the wheel is for operating the rocking grate; a lever is inserted into the hole. (AC)

Right: A view of the valve gear of a 9F, the ash pan doors are in the closed position. (IA)

Right: No. 92079 at Birkenhead, October 1966 following transfer from Bromsgrove in October 1963. No. 92079 remained at Birkenhead until withdrawal in November 1967. It is fitted with the replacement BR1G tender acquired when used on banking duties on the Lickey incline. There is no sign of the large lamp fitted at the top of the smoke box door when it worked from Bromsgrove. (AC)

Left: No. 92239 at York shed, August 1965 following transfer from Feltham (Southern Region) in September 1963. The locomotive had also been allocated to Eastleigh for working oil trains from Fawley Refinery (Southampton). AWS is fitted. (AC)

Right: As originally built (and the same as the 'Britannia' class) there were two small steps on the inside of the mainframes. This was soon modified to a single larger step seen here. Many 9F's however never received this modification. (JJ)

Right: No. 92015 at Ais Gill on the Settle Carlisle line on an 'Anhydrite' working to Widnes, October 1965. The locomotive, fitted to a BR1C tender, had been allocated to various depots on the LM region before arriving at Carlisle (Kingmoor) in July 1964. It remained there until withdrawal in April 1967. (AC)

Above:
A detail of the pony truck and buffer beam of No. 92214. The righthand pipe on the buffer beam is for steam heating and as far is known was never fitted to BR locomotives in service although the buffer beams of Western Region locomotives had a small cut-out and holes for the attachment of the steam heat pipe. (AC)

Left: No. 92008 at Birmingham (New Street) with a Leeds to Bristol train, August 1959. The locomotive at this time was allocated to Saltley (Birmingham) and is fitted with a BR1G tender. The first coach is an early LMS panelled type dating from the 1920s. (AC)

33

CHAPTER TWO

CONSTRUCTION

The 9Fs were built at Swindon and Crewe
and each batch was built for specific regions
which dictated which type of tender was fitted.

The Class was delivered against 10 different order numbers (the official terminology was Lot Numbers) and all were built at Crewe or Swindon works. Each batch of locomotives were built for specific regions which dictated which type of tender was originally fitted.

The decision to incorporate the Franco-Crosti type boiler and mechanical stoker meant that some of the class were delivered out of number sequence and Swindon appears to have been very slow in completing its last batch of locomotives. This took from September 1957 to April 1960 to complete 43 locomotives whilst Crewe only took from May to December 1958 to build its final batch of 30 (excluding the three stoker fitted locomotives built at Crewe between April and May 1958). Swindon's slow rate of build explains why No. 92220 *Evening Star* was the final steam locomotive built for British Railways and not No. 92250 completed at Crewe.

The first order (30 locomotives) for the 9F came in 1952 to be included in the 1953 build programme. By this time over 300 locomotives built to other 'Standard' designs were already in service. Before Crewe had made much progress on building this first batch, a further 67 of the class were ordered for building in the 1954 programme.

The first 10 locomotives were intended for the Western Region (WR) but only the first eight actually went to that region and all were fitted with Automatic Train Control (ATC) equipment, unique to the WR.

As each batch was built the opportunity was taken to make some design changes from batch to batch as described below. As it took six years to complete building of the class this gave sufficient time for modifications to be sketched out and implemented. The imperatives to modify were the same as they have always been, but there was a greater preparedness to actually change things for the better.

1 Items that broke, or did not work effectively included:
a Fitting ash pan hopper doors from No. 92087 (retrospectively fitted to those already built).
b Return crank fixing changed from LNER style to LMS four-bolt fixing.
c Removing the Crosti boiler water fed heaters.
d Enlarging the cutouts in the valance running plate (to improve access to the lubricators).
e Modification of the steam brake.
f Modifications to the regulator to prevent sticking open at full throttle.
g Removal of the Berkley mechanical stokers.
2 Items that could improve performance or servicing, this included fitment of the double

Above: No. 92232 at the entrance to the roundhouse at Oxley shed (Wolverhampton) in ex-works condition in the 1960s. The original BR1G tender has the late totem. The original steps under the smokebox are still fitted. (AC)

Left: No. 92022 in store at Wellingborough shed in September 1961 waiting for delivery to Crewe works to have the Crosti pre-heater removed. This was not carried out until April 1962. This meant that the locomotive had been in store since May 1959, almost three years. (CR)

A view of the firebox backhead of one of the stoker fitted 9Fs and shows the butterfly doors above the stoker to allow for hand firing when lighting up the engine and supplementing the stoker in event of a problem. This view also shows the extended cab floor fitted to all 9Fs. (IA)

chimney and changes to the lubrication system (following excessive wear to piston and valves).

Some parts of the design did not work as planned and proved troublesome in service so the design team then sketched out modifications. In some cases the modification was to change from say from an earlier LNER design to that of an earlier LMS design as in the return crank fixing.

BERKLEY MECHANICAL STOKER

Although common on US-built locomotives mechanical stokers were virtually unknown on Britain's railways, but as locomotives became larger, testing had revealed that at high power outputs the limiting factor was not the boiler but the ability of the fireman to shovel enough coal. This limit had been reached in the USA many years before, (with the much larger loading gauge leading to the production of massive articulated locomotives, with firebox capacities considerably above the ability of any fireman)

hence the development of mechanical stokers and oil firing. When operating on fast freight services the nominated capacity for a 9F was 37 wagons (each 16 tons [16,257kg]) running at 42mph (68kph). As part of the modernisation programme it was desirable to increase this to 53 wagons, however the stoking ability of a fireman needed to be addressed. Therefore proposals were made to investigate the fitting of a mechanical stoker, and subsequently three locomotives, Nos. 92165 to 92167 were selected. All were built at Crewe and entered service between April and May 1958.

The fitting of the Berkley mechanical stoker (not the most common type used in the USA) required modifications to the tender which required a new type BR1K (outwardly similar to BR1C). This type had a reduced water capacity from 4,725 down to 4,325 gallons (21,480 down to 19,662 litres).

The Berkley stoker worked by using an Archimedean-type screw below the coal space powered by a steam engine (if necessary this could be put in reverse to clear blockages). The coal

Above: The frames of No. 92000 under construction at Crewe show how the horn guides are centred in the frames. Also the substantial cast cross pieces, both of which contributed to the strength of the frames. (IA)

Number	Works	Date	Tender Type	Original Chimney	Return Crank Fixing	Comments
Nos. 92000 to 92009	Crewe	January to March 1954	BR1G	Single	LNER	Nos. 92000, 92001, 92002, 92005 and 92006 had the double chimney fitted between 1961/62 at Swindon. The first eight to the WR and the remainder to London Midland (LM) Region.
Nos. 92010 to 92014	Crewe	May 1954	BR1F	Single	LNER	To Eastern Region
Nos. 92015 to 92019	Crewe	October 1954	BR1C	Single	LNER	To LM Region
Nos. 92020 to 92029	Crewe	May to August 1955	BR1B	Crosti	LNER	Fitted with the Franco-Crosti boiler. When the Franco-Crosti equipment was removed a single chimney fitted. To LM Region.
Nos. 92030 to 92044	Crewe	November 1954 to January 1955	BR1F	Single	Mixture of LNER and LMS four bolt	To Eastern Region.
Nos. 92045 to 92059	Crewe	February to November 1955	BR1C	Single	Mixture of LNER and LMS four bolt	To LM Region.
Nos. 92060 to 92066	Crewe	November and December 1955	BR1B	Single	LMS four bolt	To Eastern Region. Air pumps fitted for Tyne Dock To Consett workings.
Nos. 92067 to 92076	Crewe	December 1955 to March 1956	BR1F	Single	LMS four bolt	To Eastern Region.
Nos. 92077 to 92086	Crewe	March to June 1956	BR1C	Single	LMS four bolt	To LM Region. No. 92079 had double chimney fitted circa 1961.
Nos. 92087 to 92096	Swindon	August 1956 to April 1957	BR1F	Single	LMS four bolt	To LM Region.
Nos. 92097 to 92099	Crewe	July and August 1956	BR1B	Single	LMS four bolt	To Eastern Region. Air pumps fitted for Tyne Dock to Consett workings.
Nos. 92100 to 92139	Crewe	August 1956 to June 1957	BR1C	Single	LMS four bolt	To LM Region.
Nos. 92140 to 92149	Crewe	June to September 1957	BR1F	Single	LMS four bolt	To Eastern Region.
Nos. 92150 to 92164	Crewe	September 1957 to April 1958	BR1C	Single	LMS four bolt	To LM Region.
Nos. 92165 to 92167	Crewe	April 1958	BR1K	Double	LMS four bolt	To LM Region. Stoker fitted tender. Double chimney fitted from new
Nos. 92168 to 92177	Crewe	December 1957 to March 1958	BR1F	Single	LMS four bolt	To Eastern Region.
Nos. 92178 to 92202	Swindon	September 1957 to December 1958	BR1F	All double except for No. 92179, No. 92180, No. 92181, No. 92182	LMS four bolt	To Eastern Region. No. 92178 was first 9F to be fitted with double chimney
Nos. 92203 to 92220	Swindon	April 1959 to March 1960	BR1G	Double	LMS four bolt	To Western Region. No. 92220 named *Evening Star*. The last steam locomotive built for BR.
Nos. 92221 to 92250	Crewe	May to December 1958	BR1G	Double	LMS four bolt	To Western Region. No. 92250 was the last steam locomotive built at Crewe works.

Right: No. 92167 departs Appleby on a Carlisle to Water Orton (Birmingham) freight in July 1961. The locomotive was still fitted with a Berkley stoker at this time and this may account for the heavy black exhaust. All the stoker fitted 9Fs were allocated to Saltley at this time specifically to work these Birmingham to Carlisle trains. (CR/DC)

was delivered to the firebox by four steam jets controlled by the fireman. From the outside it was not possible to identify the locomotive as having the stoker fitted. Following testing the three locomotives were allocated to Saltley (Birmingham) where they worked on diagrams of fast freights to Carlisle. Attempts were made to screen the coal used, as too much 'slack' would just go straight through to the chimney.

Whilst improved steam generation could be achieved it was (as expected) at the cost of higher fuel consumption but the reality was that firemen never really mastered the 'art' of using a stoker. The additional operational cost of providing the right type of coal to just three locomotives proved to be too much and

the equipment was removed in 1962. The locomotives were returned to hand firing. It is presumed that the tenders were also modified back to the original water capacity of 4,725 gallons (21,480 litres).

One of the stoker equipped locomotives, No. 92167, had the distinction of being the last 9F to be withdrawn on 29 June 1968.

FRANCO-CROSTI BOILERED LOCOMOTIVES

As part of the programme a batch of locomotives were built with water preheaters known as Franco-Crosti boilers which was an attempt by British Railways to react to the Governments

Above: No. 92000 is seen under construction showing how the platform is attached to the boiler rather than the traditional method of attaching to the top of the frames. (IA)

wish to reduce weekly coal consumption by 10,000 tons (10,160,500kg) a week. It must be remembered at the time this decision was made, the coal industry was in turmoil following Nationalisation with demand exceeding supply. The design had been developed by Attillio Franco and Piero Crosti and incorporated a secondary boiler which heated the water prior to it being injected into the main boiler. This secondary boiler used the heat from the primary boiler to pass through this secondary boiler before being ejected into the atmosphere, heating the water before it was injected into the primary boiler. The position of the preheater under the primary boiler resulted in the chimney being located along side the boiler. Various boiler schemes incorporating different designs of superheater and boiler diameter were attempted before the final design was confirmed. This had a new boiler of smaller proportions than the conventional 9F boiler to accommodate

the preheater, all within the constraints of the restrictive British loading gauge.

The Crosti-boilered locomotives looked like nothing ever seen before on the British network, with the boiler pitched as high it could possibly be, and a huge side mounted exhaust on the right of the boiler (looking forward from the cab). The high temperature feed pipe to the clack valves (one on each side of the boiler) on the side of the boiler were lagged as the temperature of the water was considerably higher than normal. In addition there was a third feed pipe and clack valve (without pre-heat), presumably as a safety feature to ensure water could be fed into the boiler in the event of any problems with the preheater. The chimney at the front in the conventional position was only used for lighting up and once the locomotive was in steam it was covered by a hinged flap which was then bolted down. To assist the shed staff to

Above: No. 92024 at Crewe works after the removal of the Crosti preheater. The sandbox fillers remain at the front. A revised step below the smokebox is fitted. The top lamp bracket has been lowered to the side of the smokebox door handle. (IA/JRC)

Left: Following the introduction of the Crosti locomotives, crews complained of smoke drifting into the cab, so the locomotives were modified with smoke deflectors. (IA/CS)

No. 92021 at Wellingborough shed in February 1960 ready to have the Crosti preheater removed. This was done at Crewe works between April and June 1960. The locomotive was then returned to Wellingborough. The LNER-style return crank fitting is retained. No. 92021 is fitted to the original BR1B tender although in later years this was changed for a BR1G tender. (AC)

access the flap a handrail was placed at the base of the chimney. In addition a long step and extra handrails were located on the fireman's side of the cab. The reversing shaft on the driver's side was parallel to the footplate unlike the sloping type on the standard locomotive. The space taken up between the frames by the preheater forced the designers to place the sandboxes on the outside of the frames including one on either side of the smoke box in front of the cylinders. One sandbox filler was fitted vertically in the platform on the fireman's side.

The additional complexity of the design meant that the allocated batch was built much later than expected and not delivered until May 1955. The attempt to reduce coal consumption using the Franco-Crosti boiler under the limitations of the British loading gauge was not a success and the subsequent removal of the equipment will be detailed later in this book.

The 20 Franco-Crosti boilered 9Fs were all allocated to Wellingborough in May 1955 where they rapidly proved to be very unpopular with crews and running staff on a number of counts, namely:

1 The crews resented the filthy working environment caused by the close proximity of the side-mounted exhaust to the cab.
2 Poor steaming compared to the standard 9F also operating from Wellingborough.
3 The complexities of having to clean two sets of tubes inside the main boiler and preheater was not popular with running staff.

As a result of these early experiences the locomotives were returned to Crewe works in late November where a number of modifications where made particularly in revised draughting arrangements with a sharper blast being incorporated in an attempt to increase the rate of steam production. In addition to the revised draughting, smoke deflectors were fitted in an attempt to reduce the amount of smoke and steam entering the cab. This failed, as generally the slow speed running of the locomotive did not generate enough airflow to have any effect. The expected coal savings did not materialise either, as after the draughting modifications coal consumption was actually higher than with the standard 9F. With the additional months in service another major problem surfaced with severe corrosion being found in the preheater caused by sulphuric acid being precipitated out of the flue gas, causing replacement components to be manufactured in chrome steel further

increasing costs. Compared to the standard design 9F the Franco-Crosti boilered locomotives also spent more time out of service and ran less miles on average, but in part this may have been the result of their unpopularity with both crews and running staff at Wellingborough shed.

Having not achieved the savings expected and being more troublesome than the standard 9F a decision was finally made to remove the preheater and refit the locomotives with a conventional-type boiler. This new boiler was slightly smaller than the type fitted to the rest of the 9F class. Wellingborough shed had pre-empted this by placing most of the class into store in early 1959. The design office at Derby works prepared drawings for the conversion and No. 92026 became the first to have the preheater removed, being out shopped in September 1959. The last No. 92022 was not converted until June 1962 (having been in storage for three years). The conversion retained the smaller boiler and the special cylinders originally fitted (retaining the distinctive cladding) but a conventional chimney was now fitted. Strangely the converted locomotives were never fitted with smoke deflectors, and due to the smaller boiler were actually classified as an 8F. Many of the converted locomotives were out shopped without a step of any description under the smokebox door (never having been originally fitted). In the case of converted No. 92024 was seen without a step in 1960 but by 1965 one had been fitted.

The fitment of these Franco-Crosti boilers was not a success but at least it was carried out in a scientific manner in a genuine attempt to reduce coal consumption.

DOUBLE CHIMNEY

All the conventional-boilered locomotives (the Crosti-boilered locomotives were fitted with a multiple blast pipe) built up to No. 92177 were fitted with a single chimney but Swindon fitted a double chimney to No. 92178 (September 1957) and then tested it to see what benefits could be achieved. A more scientific approach to blast pipe and chimney design was being undertaken at this time at Swindon by S.O. Ell and considerable improvements had been found for a number of classes including the GWR 'Manor' and the Ivatt class 4 2-6-0s. Following these successes the 9F was selected to see if improvements could be made by fitting a double chimney. The trials on No. 92178

No. 92024 in as-built condition; note the separate door for the Crosti preheater below the main smokebox door. Two of the sand box fillers have been moved to the front of the locomotive; the space they would normally occupy is filled with the preheater drum. The buffer beam is drilled with two holes for a steam heat fitting but to the author's knowledge these were never fitted. (IA)

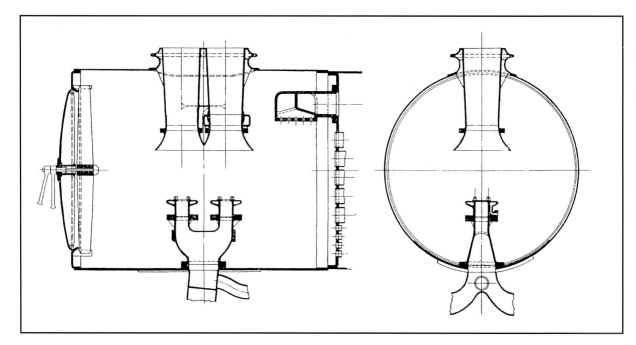

showed an increase in power output and a reduction in coal consumption.

Following this test all the subsequent locomotives built at Swindon from No. 92183 (December 1958) were fitted with a double chimney as were all the Crewe built 9Fs from No. 92221 to No. 92250. The small batch of locomotives Nos. 92179 to 92182 built at Swindon between October 1957 and December 1957 were built with a single chimney as the

trial with No. 92178 was still ongoing. Following the success of the double chimney at Swindon, the three Berkely stoker fitted examples Nos. 92165, 92166 and 92167 built at Crewe in April 1958, were also fitted with a double chimney.

Subsequently a number of WR-based locomotives were retrospectively fitted with a double chimney, these were Nos. 92000, 92001, 92002, 92005, and 92006.

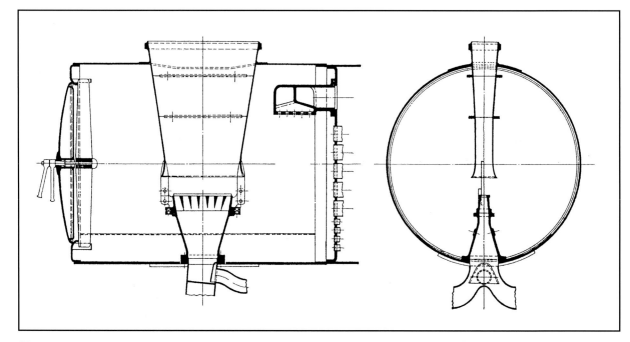

The Giesl ejector fitted to No. 92250. A standard 'Battle of Britain' class (Bulleid Pacific 4-6-2) was also fitted with a Geisl ejector. Neither class of locomotive showed enough additional economy in coal consumption to justify the cost of fitment. (IA/MM)

GIESL OBLONG EJECTOR

No. 92250 built at Crewe in December 1958 (the last steam locomotive to be built at the works) was originally fitted a with a double chimney. The locomotive was selected for the trial fitting of a Giesl oblong ejector in early 1959 (it only ran with a double chimney for five months). No. 92250 was delivered to Rugby testing station where the ejector was fitted (under the supervision of Dr Giesl). The locomotive was then tested, first with a conventional double chimney and then with the Giesl ejector.

Dr Giesl's ejector designs had been successfully applied to a large number of locomotives on the continent particularly in Austria and Germany with impressive results, giving reduced back pressure and enabling lower quality coal to be used with no loss in performance.

The reason for trying the Giesl system was to produce economies when using lower grade coal and in this respect the trial was partially successful, showing savings of between 3.8% and 8.4% over the single chimney-fitted locomotive. However the average mileage of the 9F class was falling, giving little scope for the economies to cover the cost of fitting the device to locomotives. Therefore a decision was made by BR not to fit further locomotives of the class with this device. The unique-design chimney remained on the locomotive until No. 92250 was scrapped in 1965.

In 1960 an un-rebuilt ex-Southern Railway's Bullied Light Pacific No. 34064 *Fighter Command* was also fitted with a Giesl oblong ejector but again the savings could not justify the cost of fitment. Once again a case of too little too late. It is surprising that the Giesl chimney was not tried on the Franco-Crosti boilered locomotives as this was a common combination on the continent.

The shape of a Giesl chimney was instantly recognisable when viewed from the front, it being much slimmer than a conventional type.

AIR PUMPS – CONSETT IRON ORE TRAINS

A total of 10 locomotives were ordered for the North Eastern Region specifically to work iron ore trains. These worked over a 22 mile (35.4km) line with severe gradients hauling heavy loads from the Tyne Docks to Consett steelworks. These trains used special hopper wagons with air-operated doors requiring the locomotive to provide a source of compressed air. The introduction of the 9F for both hauling the trains and as bankers enabled the capacity of the iron ore trains to rise from eight to nine fully-loaded hopper wagons. This allowed major operational efficiencies over the previous locomotives used (ex-LNER O1 2-8-0s). This may not appear to be much of an increase but iron ore is much heavier than an equivalent volume of coal, and the

Above: The fireman's side of No. 92063, one of the Tyne Dock locomotives fitted with air pumps. Note the additional air tank below the platform on the driver's side. (AC)

Below: No. 92079 fitted with a headlamp for banking duties on the Lickey incline south of Birmingham. When transferred to Bromsgrove for these duties the LM Region BR1B tender was exchanged for a WR-type BR1G. This allowed better visibility when running tender first down the bank. (IA/PJS)

loadings for a 9F were in the region of 800 tons (812,840kg) per train.

To work these services, 9Fs (Nos. 92060, 92061, 92062, 92063, 92064, 92065, 92066, 92097, 92098 and 92099) were fitted with two Westinghouse air pumps on the fireman's side of the locomotive midway between the cab and smokebox and recessed into the platform. This equipment provided compressed air to operate the hopper doors thus enabling rapid unloading and therefore a quick turnaround. This required an additional air pipe fitted to each end of the locomotive and this was much taller than the standard vacuum pipe. An additional long-shape air tank was fitted on the fireman's side of the locomotive, just below the platform again approximately midway between the cab and the smokebox.

FRONT HEADLIGHT

A 9F was transferred to Bromsgrove shed (No. 92079 in May 1956) to replace the Midland Railway 0-10-0 (known as 'Big Bertha') as the big locomotive for banking on the Lickey incline (also a number of tank locomotives used as bankers) and had the front headlight transferred from 'Big Bertha' to the 9F. The 9F retained the headlamp until 1960 but stayed as banker at Bromsgrove until October 1963 (when transferred away to Birkenhead). As part of the move to Bromsgrove shed the tender was changed from the BR1C originally fitted to a BR1G, which was the usual tender for WR locomotives and would aid visibility when running tender first back down the bank. The tender was modified at Bromsgrove with a small cut-out on the drivers side to aid hand coaling. To provide the electricity for the lamp a small steam generator was mounted below the cab on the drivers side.

The lamp was used as a safety measure when buffering up to trains in the dark and reduced the risk of hitting the rear of the train at too high a speed, but the Bromsgrove crews seemed to be adept at coupling up in the dark without using the light.

RETURN CRANK FIXING

The valve gear and motion for all the standard classes was designed at Doncaster and the 9Fs were built with an LNER-style return crank fixing (also used on the 'Britannia') but this was subsequently modified to the LMS-style four bolt fixing and it would appear that most of the class were subsequently modified to this type of fixing. I have not been able to identify at which locomotive number or batch the new build started with the four-bolt fixing but certainly most of the Crosti-boilered locomotives appeared to have the LNER-style fixing when new, although most had them changed for the LMS four-bolt type. From photographic evidence I have determined the following:

- Original LNER type, up to No. 92039.
- Mixture of two types, between Nos. 92040 and 92049.
- LMS 4 bolt type from 92050 onwards.

Despite the change to the LMS four-bolt fixing (for all new-build 9Fs from No. 92050) not all locomotives originally fitted with the LNER type were retrospectively changed, certainly No. 92000 retained this original fitting into 1962, as did No. 92029 (ex-Crosti) to 1967 and No. 92029 (ex-Crosti boiler) in 1962.

ASH PAN HOPPER DOOR

As originally built, shed workmen experienced difficulty in raking out all the ash left in the hopper so subsequently the design was changed to incorporate two additional hopper doors which resolved the problem. These doors were almost without exception left in the open position.

LUBRICATOR ACCESS

As built the front face of the lubricator was partially covered by a plate but this was subsequently removed (along the same lines as on the 'Britannia') to improve access. The change appears to have been made from locomotive No. 92030 (source Brian Reed) and all locomotives prior to this were retrospectively modified.

LAMP IRONS

As built for all the regions (except the Western Region) the 9F class was fitted with standard lamp irons. For those locomotives built for the Western their GWR-style lamp irons were fitted.

A number of the small batch of locomotives transferred to Eastleigh from the Western Region (originally with GWR-style lamp brackets) were fitted with both BR and WR lamp brackets as well as additional brackets on the smokebox door (either side of the smokebox dart) to allow the use of SR-type white discs. These include locomotives No. 92005 and No. 92239.

SMOKEBOX FRONT STEP

As originally built two steps were fixed to the inside of the mainframes below the smokebox door. The same arrangement was fitted to the original 'Britannia' class and were subsequently modified, as with the 'Britannia' class the steps were revised. This involved removing the two steps and fitting a much larger single step, with a central support bracket, which covered the space between the front frames. As with the 'Britannia' this appears to have been a slow process as many of the class were scrapped with the original step arrangements still in place.

In the case of the ex-Crosti boilered locomotives when originally built there were no front steps (to allow access to the preheater drum door) but when the locomotives were rebuilt all were fitted, over a period, with the revised step arrangement. Nos. 92022, 92024, 92027 and 92028 were observed with the revised central step but No. 92025 did not appear to have been fitted with any steps following the removal of the Crosti preheater.

ATC & AWS EQUIPMENT

When built the class was not fitted with British Railway's Automatic Warning System (AWS) but those allocated to the Western Region were fitted with Automatic Train Control (ATC) and fitted at Swindon works following delivery of the first locomotive from Crewe works.

The ATC equipment could be identified by the following:

1 Battery box under the cab (left-hand side [from the front] only) The box was at 90^0 to the frames.
2 Pipe (Conduit) along the whole length of the bottom edge of the platform (sometimes passing under the lubricator).
3 No 'bash' plate under the front buffer beam.
4 A circular fitting on the top of the exhaust

ejector (the ejector being located adjacent to the rear edge of the drivers side smoke deflector).

ATC was originally fitted to Nos. 92000, 92001, 92003, 92004, 92005, 92006 and 92007. Nos. 92221 to 92250. Nos. 92203 to 92220. Nos. 92236, 92241, 92245 and 92248.

In line with most of the modern BR locomotives in traffic, a decision was made to fit a standard automatic warning system (AWS). In practice, as with many other classes this was a haphazard affair and the majority of the 9Fs were never equipped. However from observations and analysing photographs a number of 9Fs were fitted with AWS and the identified locomotives are as follows: Nos. 92020, 92033, 92034, 92035, 92037, 92038, 92039, 92040, 92041, 92042, 92043 and 92049.

Nos. 92060, 92061, 92062, 92063, 92064, 92065, 92066 and 92069. Nos. 92076, 92077 and 92078. Nos. 92092, 92094 and 92097.

Nos. 92128, 92177, 92178, 92183, 92191 and 92211.

The system was similar in principle to the ATC system and could be identified by:

1 Revised battery position under the cab, the battery now angled.

2 Small air cylinder attached to the main frame under the cab.

3 AWS 'bash' plate below front buffer beam. Sometimes the brackets to attach the 'bash' plate were on the front face of the buffer beam and sometimes behind.

4 Conduit along the bottom of the cab and along the bottom edge of the platform (similar to the ATC conduit)

5 A small circular-shaped contact shoe under the leading pony truck.

All of the locomotives so fitted were at the time of fitment allocated to the Eastern Region including the allocations at Annesley, Doncaster, and Langworth Junction.

Above: No. 92178 fitted with AWS equipment, the air tank with battery box is under the cab and the conduit clipped to the underside of the footplate. This locomotive was the first to be fitted with the double chimney and was only ever allocated to the Eastern Region. (IA)

CHAPTER THREE

IN SERVICE

By 1958 the 9Fs were working in three regions of BR
and were highly regarded by both operating staff and crews.

Like 'Britannia' locomotives the initial introduction of the class into service was not without incident. Problems with the steam brakes and regulators resulted in a number of the early locomotives to be involved in minor collisions. Both problems were soon resolved and the locomotives were soon hard at work on freight services.

After the first batch of 9Fs went to Newport, subsequent batches went to Wellingborough, Toton, Kettering and Leicester (Midland). Those at Cricklewood (on the Midland main line) were used on both coal trains and fast freights from the East Midlands to London. Similarly the batch sent to Annesley, Peterborough (New England) and March on the Eastern Region were used on coal or fast freight, exactly the services for which the 9F had been designed. A small batch was sent to Bidston shed (near Birkenhead) to work the iron ore trains from the docks up to John Summers steelworks at Shotton (on the Wirral). Birkenhead-based locomotives took over these workings when Bidston shed closed.

By 1958 the 9F class locomotives were working hard in three regions of BR and were highly regarded by all the crews, even those on the Western Region. From the shedmaster's point of view the 9F was an excellent locomotive (with the notable exception of the Crosti-boilered examples) with few problems for the shed fitters and none for the crews. The one feature disliked (this also applied to the 'Britannia' class) was the 'mangle'-style reversing wheel but this was a minor issue, outweighed by the 9F's virtues.

None of the class was ever allocated to Scotland but when a number were allocated to Carlisle (Kingmoor), 9Fs could regularly be seen working up to Glasgow with freight trains. The locomotives returned with empty heavy stock trains for the 'Glasgow Fortnight' holiday trains down to Blackpool.

The class was particularly associated with iron ore workings, such as the Tyne Dock to Consett, the Bidston Dock to John Summers steelworks (on the Wirral) and iron ore trains in the East Midlands with much of the traffic going to Corby steelworks. The line from Newport Docks up to the steel works at Ebbw Vale had severe gradients over the 20 mile (32km) length and perfectly suited the 9F. The locomotive's sure footedness and good steaming ability made even the GWR staff like them!

The class was also long associated with the Long Meg (on the Settle-Carlisle line) 'Anhydryte' trains which supplied an important raw material to the chemical industry. This was as a long distance service which started near Penrith on the heavily graded Settle-Carlisle line and ended at Widnes on the River Mersey.

Above:
No. 92073 displaying an express passenger head code when pulling a summer Bradford to Poole train, August 1963. The locomotive has a BR1F tender and was allocated to 16D (Annesley) shed in early 1957. (CR)

Left: No. 92001 at Midsomer Norton on the S&D line with a summer Nottingham to Bournemouth (West) passenger train. The locomotive was at Bath (Green Park) in the summers of 1961 and 1962. No. 92001 remained on the WR until November 1966 and was then moved to Wakefield. The locomotive is fitted to a BR1G tender but received a BR1F in 1965. (CR/PAF)

The smooth ride, steaming capacity and ability to pull heavy trains at a good speed soon brought the 9Fs to the attention of hard pressed depot foremen who were looking for locomotives to work summer Saturday trains. At the summer peak many shed masters could look out onto the yard and find no locomotives left for the extra holiday trains, so it was not surprising to find 9Fs working summer extra trains and once crews (and shed foremen) realised the 9F could run happily well past the design limit of 50mph (80.5kph) the class began to appear regularly on passenger trains.

The passengers, presumably, were more impressed with a 9F on the front of their holiday extra rather than the sight of a scruffy 4F 0-6-0!

From 1957, a number of routes saw examples of 9F–hauled summer Saturday trains including Sheffield Midland to Bangor, North Wales; Leicester to Hastings, Sussex (the locomotive would be changed at Willesden); Leicester to Paignton (locomotive change at Bristol); Manchester to Blackpool, Southport and Fleetwood.

Once crews and shedmasters had witnessed at first hand the utility of the 9F it did not take long before the class began to appear on regular passenger services. From 1955, there had been isolated examples of a 9F being substituted for a failed passenger locomotives. With the increasing number of 9Fs being delivered, the number of instances of locomotives being diagrammed for passenger workings increased. On the Great Central line the large number of 9Fs at Annesley began to make appearances on express passenger services including the 'South Yorkshireman' complete with headboard.

In the summer of 1958 the Eastern Region also began to diagram 9Fs on passenger trains, partly prompted by a shortage of available express passenger locomotives. Initially 9F locomotives were only used on five coach semi-fast trains to Peterborough. The return working was an express so unless the shed master at Grantham could provide a substitute locomotive the 9F was used for this working. In August 1958, No. 92184 was timed at 90mph (145kph) with a 14-coach express between Peterborough and Kings Cross, this being the highest recorded speed for a 9F.

The Western Region received the allocation of 9Fs later than the other regions and did not start to use 9F on passenger trains until the summer of 1959. This commenced

with summer holiday passenger trains but soon moved to diagrammed workings with No. 92206 heading the Plymouth to Paddington ('The Mayflower') express service in August 1959. The Western Region of course were used to using big locomotives on the summer passenger services (47xx class 2-8-0 being regulars) so moving up to a 9F was not such a big step. Once No. 92220 *Evening Star* had been allocated to Cardiff (Canton) in 1960 it did not take long for the class to appear on passenger workings. No. 92220 was regularly on Cardiff to Portsmouth trains but following the failure of a booked 'Britannia' class *Evening Star* was used on the Cardiff to Paddington 'Red Dragon' service, returning later that day with the 'Capitals United Express' (*see title spread*). This was repeated a number of times. However as with the Eastern Region some concern was registered and the regular use of 9Fs on fast express services to Paddington was not acceptable.

The authorities became concerned about the excessive wear to piston and valve rings and tried to dissuade shedmasters from the use of 9Fs on passenger trains but stopped short of an absolute ban. The result was that the 9F continued to be used on passenger services

usually on summer holiday trains (the absence of steam heating preventing all but emergency use during the winter).

However the use on passenger trains at lower speed and on hilly routes was a different matter. In March 1960 trials were conducted on the Somerset & Dorset line with No. 92204 (with 10 coaches) to ascertain if the 9Fs could be used on the heavy summer express return services between Bath and Bournemouth. The trials (conducted in heavy rain) were a resounding success. In July 1960 four 9Fs (No. 92203, 92204, 92205 and 92206 all from 82B Bristol (St Phillips Marsh), were transferred to Bath shed in preparation for working the many heavy summer Saturday through trains. These included the 'Pines Express' a Manchester to Bournemouth service, also the Bradford to Bournemouth train. The locomotives were ideally suited to the route, generally improved punctuality and reduced the number of double headed workings required. At the end of the summer traffic the locomotives were moved away but another batch of four returned for the summer of 1961 (Nos. 92000, 92001, 92006 and 92112). In 1962, Nos. 92001, 92210, 92233 and 92245 were used; in 1963 Nos. 92224 and 92220, and

Above: No. 92113 answers a shed-masters prayer by hauling a Sheffield to Blackpool summer special in July 1958. The locomotive looks in total control of the train giving the crew an easier time than if they had been given a run down 4F. This may have been the case in earlier years. (AC)

An overhead vew of No. 92212 when running on the Great Central Railway showing the recessed safety valves and compact dome cover. (AC)

No. 92137 travels through Rotherham (Masborough) in October 1963 with a freight and passes D108 (Class 45) on a passenger train. Baskets of racing pigeons wait on the platform along with the passengers. (CR/GW)

Allocations

December 1957		December 1960		1965		1968	
17B Burton	2	86A Newport	10	8C Speke Jnct	9	10A Carnforth	10
18B Westhouses	7	86C Cardiff	2	8H Birkenhead	54	8C Speke Jnct	7
15B Kettering	4	81C Southall	4	12A Carlisle	14		
18A Toton	24	17C Rowsley	6	2D Banbury	17		
14A Cricklewood	4	16D Annesley	31	50A York	8		
6F Bidston	3	26A Newton Heath	4	88A Cardiff (Canton)	4		
15C Leicester (M)	2	15A Wellingborough	28	85B Gloucester	3		
86A Newport	8	15B Kettering	7	9D Newton Heath	11		
21A Saltley	20	34E New England	30	2E Saltley	11		
38B Annersley	30	40B Immingham	7	1E Northampton	1		
15A Wellingborough	26	6F Bidston	3	40B Immingham	11		
35A New England	21	18A Toton	13	41J Langwith Jnct	17		
21C Bromsgrove	1	14A Cricklewood	1	8B Warrington	15		
		52H Tyne Dock	10	52H Tyne Dock	10		
		85D Bromsgrove	1	16C Derby	2		
		18B Westhouses	7	2A Tyseley	7		
		15C Leicester (Mid)	15	40E Colwick	7		
		21A Saltley	13	34E New England	3		
		36A Doncaster	18	36A Doncaster	7		
		81A Old Oak	3	36C Froddingham	1		
		82D Westbury	3	86B Newport	4		
		83D Plymouth (Laira)	1	86E Severn Tunnel Jnct	7		
		82E Bristol (Barrow Rd)	3	81C Southall	4		
		84C Banbury	9	82E Bristol (Barrow Rd)	2		
		82B St Phillips Marsh	2				

Note: **Bold numeral** indicates the number of locomotives allocated.

in 1964 Nos. 92214 and 92226. All the locomotives allocated to Bath shed for these summer services were fitted with the double chimney. No. 92220 *Evening Star* had the privilege of running the last 'Pines Express' service on this route before closure and the service being used elsewhere.

ROUTES

Like many classes the 9F was associated with specific routes and workings even though the class was common across much of the BR network.

The 'windcutter' (also known as 'runners' because of running speed) coal trains between the Nottingham coalfields and Woodford Halse (in Northamptonshire) operated by 9Fs from Annesley shed are a good example of the class enabling new traffic to be generated. The 9F enabled a speeding-up of the many daily coal trains allowing daily return trips to be made with the trains almost being run like passenger trains. At Woodford Halse the coal would travel on to London or to a steelworks in South Wales.

The higher-speed running meant that the locomotives could run 300 return trips per annum, which by steam standards was very intensive working.

In January 1961 three 9Fs (Nos. 92205, 92206 and 92231) were allocated to Eastleigh shed (code 71A) on the Southern Region for working heavy (1,200 tons [1,219,260kg]) oil trains from the Fawley oil refinery (located on Southampton Water) to the Midlands. In August 1961 a further two locomotives (Nos. 92211 and 92239) joined the Eastleigh allocation.

Subsequently a small number of 9Fs were allocated to Feltham shed (code 70D) on the Southern, No. 92205 (June 1963), No. 92231 (January 1963) and No. 92239 (June 1963). The locomotives remained only for a few months before being reallocated to York (code 50A).

By the mid-1960s the 9Fs were allocated mainly to the Midland and Eastern regions. A large number were located at Birkenhead, and the author visited Birkenhead shed one summer evening in 1966 where he saw row after row of 9Fs waiting for the next day's working – very atmospheric!

ALLOCATIONS

Plymouth (Laira) received a small allocation in 1960 (Nos. 92209 and 92249) but the locomotives were moved away after a few months.

As mentioned in the section on routes worked, the 9F revolutionised the working of fast coal trains on the Great Central main line when a batch were allocated to Annesley shed (north of Nottingham). The shed was adjacent to a large marshalling yard where loaded coal wagons from the many collieries in the North Nottingham coalfields were made up into trains for shipment south. The first 9F allocated to Annesley was No. 92010 in March 1956 when it was loaned from March shed for trials. The trials were eminently successful and in February 1957, No. 92010 returned to Annesley closely followed in March by nine locomotives from Doncaster shed followed by a further 11 locomotives (from March shed) in the same month. By 1958, there were 30 of the class allocated to the shed. At that time this was the largest allocation of the class.

A strange anomaly was the sighting in July 1964, at Nottingham (Victoria) of No. 92120 officially allocated to Leicester (Midland) fitted with a 5A Crewe (North) shed plate when working a Saturday Poole to Sheffield passenger train. No 9Fs were officially allocated to Crewe (North) so why it was fitted with this shed plate is a mystery?

REPAIR LOCATIONS

The main works for heavy repairs were: **Crewe, Swindon** and **Darlington.** The works became responsible for the overhauls of the 9F. Following the allocation to the North Eastern region locomotives to Tyne Dock shed and also shared 9F work with Doncaster for the Eastern Region (No. 92011 in 1957). The first 9F to visit Darlington was No. 92036 in May 1955, a light casual repair for accident damage. Following the closure of Doncaster works (November 1963) and a change of policy to move some steam overhaul work from Crewe (to allow the building of Diesels) to Darlington. 9Fs from other regions were overhauled there until the works closed in February 1965. Work was also carried out at Eastleigh.

Above: No. 92212 hauling a train of soda ash wagons in July 1967. This was exactly the type of train the 9F was designed for, heavy services running at higher speeds. Even as late as 1967 the locomotive is steam tight and the safety valves are feathering. The smokebox number plate is missing. (IA/GPC)

Above: No. 92001 at Oxford with an express passenger train (from Bournemouth [West] to Newcastle), August 1965. The locomotive is fitted with a double chimney and has a BR1F tender replacing the original BR1G. Western Region ATC equipment is retained. (CR)

Right: No. 92140 on a fully-fitted fish train running as an express freight in August 1961. The locomotive at this time was allocated to Peterborough (New England) and is in the usual 'care worn' condition. (CR)

Above: No. 92056 on the Settle-Carlisle line with empties returning to Long Meg quarries in July 1967. The locomotive at this time was allocated to Carlisle (Kingmoor) shed and retains the BR1C tender. The locomotive was withdrawn in November 1967. (CR)

Left: No. 92156 on the West Coast main line at Tebay (Cumbria) passing the locomotive depot. The locomotive was only ever allocated to two depots, Toton up to March 1965 and then Warrington. (CR)

No. 92240 under repair at Crewe works in the 1960s. An 81C Southall shed plate and GWR-style lamp irons are fitted. ATC is fitted, identified by the circular fitment on top of the exhaust ejector (just behind the cutout for the steam pipe). (IA/RW)

Eastleigh. As with Darlington, the works only became responsible for 9F overhauls when some of the class were allocated to the local shed and when some steam work was moved from Crewe. Also due to the closure of works such as Gorton and Horwich. Locomotives seen at Eastleigh include No. 92004 (1962), No. 92029 (1964 light casual), No. 92053 (1964), No. 92116 (1964) and No. 92138 (1964).

As with a number of steam classes the 9F could be seen at other works usually for non-classified or emergency repairs. Examples include:

Gorton. No. 92000 (December 1962), No. 92043 (1960 light casual) and No. 92045 (1962)

Stratford. No. 92014 (1957) and No. 92044 (1955 non-classified)

Rugby. No. 92010 (1959)

Caerphilly. No. 92001(1961 light classified), No. 92003 (1962 light classified), No. 92236 (1962 heavy repair), No. 92246 (light casual)

Wolverhampton. No. 92227 (1962 heavy intermediate) and No. 92239 (1961 light casual)

Derby. No. 92009 (1955) and No. 92021 (1961)

Oswestry. No. 92247 (1962)

Tysley (Birmingham). No. 92219 (1962)

Above: No. 92220 *Evening Star* resplendent in lined BR Green livery on a WR express . When allocated to Cardiff (Canton) the locomotive was used on express passenger service for a period. Whoever coaled the locomotive did good job as the heap only just clears the underside of the bridge. (AC)

Left: No. 92249 descending Beattock (between Glasgow and Carlisle) with an empty stock train for 'Glasgow Fairs' holidays (the trains running between Glasgow and Blackpool) on 1 August 1964. No. 92249 has a Carlisle (Kingmoor) shed plate. The modified step below the smokebox is fitted. Whilst none of the class was allocated to Scotland, the Carlisle examples could be regularly seen working on the Scottish Region up to Glasgow. (IA/PR)

Right: No. 92085 at Oxley (Wolverhampton) roundhouse in August 1964 when the locomotive was allocated to Tyseley (Birmingham). The tender is a BR1C as the locomotive was originally allocated to the Midland Region at Wellingborough. The tender was subsequently changed to a BR1F when at Birkenhead, December 1966. (CR)

The works used for these non-classified repairs were usually close to the sheds which the 9Fs were allocated to and prevented long trips back to Crewe or Swindon for minor attention.

WITHDRAWALS

Despite the fact that most 9Fs were only a few years old, the Eastern region was the first to withdraw the class with Nos. 92170, 92175 and 92177 from Doncaster; Nos. 92171 and 92176 from Peterborough (New England) at the end of May 1964. No. 92170 being only six-years old. As mentioned elsewhere No. 92177 was actually at Crewe works for a scheduled overhaul but when partially stripped it was found that the repair could not be justified and the locomotive

was scrapped. From that date, a small number of 9Fs were withdrawn every year either because of expensive repairs or that the traffic requirements dictated the locomotive was no longer needed. It should be remembered that from the late 1950s onward BR was steadily losing freight traffic of all types to competition from road services. The last operational 9Fs were withdrawn from Carnforth shed (Lancashire) in July 1968 with the remainder of BR's steam fleet (some Black 5s and the 'Britannia' class *Oliver Cromwell*) being withdrawn a few weeks later in August 1968.

DISPOSAL

The bulk of the class survived until 1964 by which time a change of policy by BR resulted

Right: No. 92180 at Peterborough (New England) coaling stage in April 1963. The locomotive has a battery box and air tank under the cab, a 'bash' plate behind the front coupling. This indicates that AWS is fitted. A BR1F tender is fitted, usual for an Eastern Region 9F. Alongside is one of the small number of V2s modified to a double chimney in the early 1960s. (CR)

in the majority of steam locomotives being dismantled at private scrap yards rather than in BR workshops. This resulted in only one 9F being scrapped by a BR workshop this being No. 92177. This presumably was the result of a major problem being identified on the locomotive when it was inspected before the repairs commenced. This was not an unusual occurrence during the early 1960s. As an example, a Jubilee 4-6-0 was observed partially stripped for overhaul at Crewe but was withdrawn when major cracks in the mainframe were identified. In total 23 private yards scrapped 9Fs with six of them taking just one locomotive each. Only nine yards achieved double figures but three of the larger scrapyards accounted for

42% of the total. The larger scrapyards totals include:

Campbells, Airdrie, Scotland	33
Ward's, Beighton, Sheffield	34
Drapers, Hull	38
Cashmores, Newport, South Wales	21
Wards, Killmarsh, Sheffield	16

A small number of 9Fs made it to the safe haven of Woodhams at Barry Island, South Wales but this was only a reprieve for No. 92085, which was finally cut up in July 1980 having spent nearly 14 years at Woodhams. This was just four years longer than the locomotive's working life (from 1956 to withdrawal in 1966), but the remainder of 9Fs at Barry have been preserved.

Right: No. 92250 is seen on a long train of oil tanks some time between December 1963 and June 1964 when it was allocated to Newport (Ebbw Junct). The locomotive was originally built with a double chimney but received its Giesl ejector a few months later and retained this until withdrawal in December 1965. No. 92250 had the distinction of being the last steam locomotive built at Crewe works. (AC)

Right: No. 92231 was one of the small number of 9Fs allocated to the SR and carries a 71A Eastleigh shed plate. Modified lamp brackets are fitted either side of the smokebox door handle to allow the fitment of SR-type white discs. The locomotive is also fitted with AWS. (AC)

Above: No. 92245 at Southall shed on the Western Region, November 1963. No. 92245 retains the original BR1G tender and is fitted with Western Region ATC equipment. The dark area at the bottom of the tender is caused by the very cold air temperature and shows the level of water in the tender. (CR/CGS)

Left: No. 92021 at Crewe in ex-works condition in 1962. The tender is a BR1B fitted from new but subsequently changed to a BR1G in 1965. The tender also has yellow axle box covers with a red stripe. The locomotive had the Crosti pre-heater removed in 1961. This is a rare view of a clean member of this sub-class. (CR)

CHAPTER FOUR

TENDERS

There were seven types of tender and each
of the receiving regions requested a tender of a
specific type to match their proposed workings.

The tenders for the 9F class were a combination of new designs and types already existing within the range of standard tenders already in service. All the tenders shared the same wheels, underframe, wheelbase and all were fitted with roller bearings.

Each of the operating regions designated a tender of a specific type in an attempt to match proposed train workings. As an example, the Western Region specified the BR1G tender whilst the Eastern Region requested the BR1F type. Five different types of standard tenders were fitted to the class as follows:

Type		BR1B	BR1C	BR1F	BR1G	BR1K
Coal –	Tons	7	9	7	7	9
	kg	(7,112.4)	(9,114.5)	(7,112.4)	(7,112.4)	(9,114.5)
Water –	Gallons	4,725	4,725	5,625	5,000	4,325
	litres	(21,480)	(21,480)	(25,571.3)	(22,730)	(19,661.5)
Weight –	Tons	51.25	53.25	55.25	52.50	52.35
	kg	(52,073)	(54,105)	(56,137)	(53,343)	(53,190)

The basic BR standard tender was the BR1 with narrow coal bunker and introduced in 1951. Originally coupled to the 'Britannia' class locomotives the tender had a 4,250 gallons (19,321litre) water and 7 tons (7,112.4kg) of coal capacity. However it soon became evident that water capacity was marginal and this led to the development of the BR1A tender. This allowed an increase to give 5,000 gallons (22,730 litre)water capacity. The distinguishing feature of the BR1A was a much taller dome at the rear of the coal space. This tender was intended

to be fitted to the first 9Fs. However the tender design had to be modified to allow the fitment of a conventional fall plate on the tender to cover the gap on with the extended cab floor. This revised tender was designated BR1G and, except for the changes to the fall plate, it was identical to the BR1A.

BR1G

This type was originally fitted to the first ten 9Fs built and was the preferred tender for WR

Above: No. 92090 at Annesley shed (between Nottingham and Mansfield) in August 1964. The clear gap between the boiler and running gear gave cause to the nickname 'spaceships'. The locomotive is still fitted with the original BR1F tender (although No. 92090 subsequently ran with a BR1G and BR1C types). (AC)

Left: No. 92002 at Aberbyg on the line between Newport and Ebbw Vale in April 1962. The BR1G tender was retained throughout the locomotive's service life. The first eight 9Fs were allocated to Newport (Ebbw Junct) for working the heavy iron ore trains from the docks up to the steelworks. (CR)

allocated locomotives. The tender had improved visibility when running tender first. As in the case of the iron ore trains up to the steelworks at Ebbw Vale which meant running tender first with empty hoppers on the return journey.

BR1F

This tender was the one preferred by the Eastern Region and had 7 ton (7,112.4kg) coal capacity but with increased water capacity of 5,625 gallons (25,571.3 litre) and first appeared behind Nos. 92010 to 92014.

BR1B

These were fitted to the majority of the class and had 7 ton (7,112.4kg) coal capacity with 4,725 gallons (21,480 litre) water capacity and had a Stanier 'look' being very similar in appearance to

the last tenders built by the LMS for the Class 5, and for the final two 'Coronation' Pacifics.

BR1C

The only difference was the coal capacity, of 9 tons (9,114.5kg) against the 7 tons (7,112.4kg) of the BR1B. Both tenders looked identical except for the additional coal space partition plate on the BR1B which reduced coal capacity.

BR1K

The three tenders of this type were essentially identical to the BR1C but were fitted with the US-built Berkley mechanical stoker and were fitted behind Nos. 92165, 92166 and 92167. The Berkley stoker was fitted in the floor of the tender and thus reduced water capacity to 4,325 gallons (19,661.5 litre).

Left: No. 92043 with a BR1F tender, the type as fitted to 9Fs delivered to the Eastern Region. (AC)

Below: No. 92021, the original BR1B tender was exchanged for a BR1G type some time in 1965. Tender exchanges were common on 9Fs as the steam fleet was running down. The changes occured at both depots and main works to keep an operational fleet running. (IA/IGH)

Right: No. 92028 at Wellingborough shed in May 1958 before the removal of the Crosti preheater in December 1959. The locomotive was one of the 9Fs given overhauls at Eastleigh works in 1964. The BR1B tender was the type originally fitted. (AC)

Right: The rear BR1F tender showing the substantial brackets between the buffer beam and tender tank. The BR1F tender was attached to locomotives built for the Eastern Region. In preservation the tender has been fitted with steam heat indicated by the pipe to the right of the coupling. (AC)

Far right: This view clearly shows the combination of extended footplate floor and the use of a small fallplate from the tender. The fallplate partly addressed the problem of excessive draughts in the cab found on the 'Britannia' class. (AC)

Above: No. 92025 at Oxford shed fitted to a BR1B tender, July 1965. Note the yellow painted tender axle-box covers (without red stripes). The Crosti preheater was removed at Crewe works, April 1960. (CR)

Left: No. 92139 at Manchester (Victoria) on a passenger train. The tender is a BR1C, note the axle-box covers are painted yellow. (AC)

Number	Date Observed	Original Tender	Changed Tender	Comment
No. 92001	1964/1965	BR1G	BR1F	
No. 92009	1966	BR1G	BR1C	
No. 92021	1965 to 1967	BR1B	BR1G	
No. 92023	1966	BR1C	BR1G	
No. 92024	1965	BR1C	BR1G	
No. 92024	1966	BR1C	BR1F	The replacement BR1G was then changed for the BR1F
No. 92079	1956 onwards	BR1C	BR1G	Exchanged when being used as Lickey Banker to improve visibility when running in reverse.
No. 92087	1961	BR1F	BR1C	
No. 92090	1965	BR1F	BR1G	
No. 92090	1967	BR1F	BR1C	Following the change to BR1G subsequently a further change to BR1C
No. 92092	1962 onwards	BR1F	BR1C	
No. 92094	1960	BR1F	BR1C	Refitted with a BR1F in 1961 and then re acquired a BR1C in 1966.
No. 92101	1967	BR1C	BR1G	
No. 92118	1967	BR1C	BR1G	
No. 92208	1965 to 1967	BR1G	BR1C	
No. 92215	1967	BR1G	BR1B	
No. 92218	1966	BR1G	BR1C or B	
No. 92231	No date identified	BR1G	BR1C	
No. 92249	1967	BR1G	BR1B	

Having gone to great lengths to match tenders to the receiving region subsequent transfers meant that the same depot could have 9Fs with different tender type.

Tender Exchanges

As with many other classes of locomotive in the dying days of steam, depots would make tender exchanges to keep locomotives in traffic and the 9Fs were no exception. Annesley shed appears to have been quite adept at swapping tenders. Some of the tender exchanges took place at Crewe works when locomotives were overhauled, it being quicker to refurbish a tender. Some examples of known exchanges are listed opposite (although this list is not exhaustive), the keen eyed will notice that No. 92024 managed to run with three different tender types in service, as did No. 92090.

LIVERIES & NAMES

With the exception of No. 92220 *Evening Star* which
was painted in full passenger BR lined green livery,
all the class were painted plain black.

With the exception of No. 92220 *Evening Star* which was finished in BR full passenger green livery, all of the class were painted in plain black. The cab side numerals were in cream being 8in (20.3cm) tall, although locomotives overhauled at Darlington and Eastleigh subsequently received 10in (25.4cm) size numerals. For locomotives built up to 1957 the BR totem on the tender was the early (large) type. For those locomotives built in early 1957 and onwards the totem was the later (small) type. I have been unable to find the first known example of a 9F with the later totem but certainly No. 92126 built at Crewe, March 1957 was finished with the early version. As with other classes the early totem could still be seen on locomotives as late as 1965. Examples include No. 92019 in 1960.

In preservation No. 92203 was painted in BR mixed-traffic livery lined out in grey and red for a short period.

LARGE CABSIDE NUMBERS

Those locomotives receiving overhauls and repaints on the Eastern Region (at Darlington) were finished with larger cab side numerals (10in [25.4cm] instead of the normal 8in [20.3cm]). Examples include Nos. 92011,

92037, 92038, 92039, 92042, 92061 and 92089. Nos. 92140, 92170, 92180, 92185, 92186, 92190 and 92191.

Eastleigh works also used larger cab side numerals on some of the 9Fs overhauled there in the early 1960s.

POWER CLASSIFICATION

The usual 'branding' for the cab side of the class was 9F. However most of the locomotives built in the Nos. 92200 to 92250 series only had the numeral '9' on the cabside but just to make life difficult No. 92226 had 9F on the cabside from new. The use of 9 instead of 9F appears to be random with No. 92006 receiving this. No. 92087 was 9 when built but 9F in 1963.

'ROUTE AVAILABILITY' INDICATOR, WESTERN REGION

On the Western Region all locomotives carried a coloured 'spot' (approx $4^1/_2$in [11.4cm] in diameter) below the number on the cabside indicating what routes the locomotives were allowed to work. On the 9Fs this 'spot' was pale Blue (not yellow as suggested in a recent book on the 9F). Interestingly Swindon works remembered not to place this indicator on the cabside when 9Fs were built for the Eastern

Above: No. 92220 *Evening Star* in September 1962 displays a Bath 82F shed plate. No. 92220 was allocated there for working heavy summer express services on the S&D line. Following a move to Old Oak Common in October 1962, *Evening Star* returned to Bath (Green Park) for a final time in the summer of 1963. The original steps below the smoke box are retained. ATC equipment is fitted. (CR)

Left: No. 92006 in March 1965. Note the blue background to the smokebox number plate and the shed name 'York' painted on the buffer beam. The locomotive was initially allocated to the WR and was transferred to York in September 1963. (AC)

No. 92208 at Crewe South depot in August 1967 displaying a Carlisle (Kingmoor) 12A shed plate and a home made smokebox number plate. The Western Region ATC fitment is evidenced by the circular fitting on top of the exhaust ejector. (IA/NEP)

Region. When the 9Fs left the Western Region these route indicators were left on, but would be lost at the next repaint. Although difficult to see under the filth and grime No. 92208 still had the route indicator visible in August 1967 having been transferred from the Western Region (to the LM) in June 1964.

OVERHEAD WARNING INDICATORS

From April 1960, following continental practice, BR ordered the fitting of white enamel plates with the symbolic warning sign of forked lightning (in red) to strategic positions on the boiler cladding. These plates were to warn locomotive crews of the proximity of overhead wires. As the use of overhead power lines for electrification extended there were a number of accidents where personnel came into contact with the lines when either trimming coal, filling the tender or fitting lamps. The position of these warning flashes varied from locomotive to locomotive, but the usual placing were as follows:

a On the smoke deflectors near the bottom handrail

b Rear of the tender
c On the firebox sides
d On the boiler sides

TENDER AXLEBOX COVERS

When built, axlebox covers on the tenders were painted black. In common with all the BR 'Standard' classes, roller bearings were fitted. However, to indicate to shed staff that the tenders had roller bearings and to differentiate them from plain bearings the axlebox covers were subsequently painted yellow. When the type of lubrication changed, this was indicated to maintenance staff by painting the axlebox cover yellow with a horizontal red stripe. In reality this appears to have been a random treatment as I have colour photographs clearly showing plain yellow as follows: 1963 (No. 92110), 1964 (No. 92001), 1965 (No. 92025) and 1966 (No. 92223). Examples in yellow with a red stripe as follows: 1960 (No. 92019), 1962 (No. 92021) and 1963 (No. 92201). However in the majority of cases the colour of the axlebox covers is impossible to determine under the general covering of grime and filth – even where the locomotive was in reasonably

Above: The name plate and commemorative plaque on No. 92220 *Evening Star.* (AC)

clean condition the axlebox covers always appear to be liberally coated in oil.

SMOKEBOX NUMBER PLATE

In the last days of steam from 1966 onwards many locomotives were seen without smoke-box number plate. These included No. 92004 (1968), No. 92024 (1967), No. 92101 (1967), No. 92102 (1967), No. 92115 (1967), No. 92126 (1966), No. 92132 (1967) and No. 92167 (1967). Other locomotives had replacement plates made at the depot (usually from wood and with hand-painted numerals), examples included No. 92051 (in 1967), No. 92118, No. 92167 (in 1968), No. 92208 (1967) and No. 92249 (1967) or in some cases the number was chalked in the space once occupied by the smokebox plate as on No. 92004 seen in 1966.

PLAQUES & EMBELLISHMENTS

The only locomotive officially named in BR service was No. 92220 *Evening Star*. The name was the result of a challenge issued by the Western Region to its staff to suggest a name.

The successful name made reference to *North Star*, first locomotive built at Swindon. The locomotive also carried a commemorative plaque below the name plate.

However No. 92203 following preservation has carried the name plate *Black Prince* on the smoke deflectors and retained BR Black livery. At one point raised cab side numerals were fitted.

In the late days of steam unofficial names were chalked on the smoke deflectors, with varying degrees of neatness!

Many depots painted the shed name on the buffer beam but this practice was rare with 9Fs. However, No. 92113 was seen in 1966 with its shed name Birkenhead painted in full on the buffer beam, and No. 92006 was also observed with 'York' painted on the buffer beam.

A number of Scottish based locomotives of other classes often received a pale blue back-ground to the smokebox number plate and name plate. No. 92006 was seen with a pale blue background to the smokebox number plate, and it is assumed that this was applied at Carlisle (Kingmoor) shed which for a long time was part of the Scottish Region even though the locomotive was never allocated to the shed.

REVERSER ROD COVER PLATE

As built, all members of the class had the reverser rod emerge from the cab front at an angle and cut through the platform to the valve gear. A number of Western Region based locomotives were modified with a flat cover plate over the reverser shaft in front of the cab. This is presumed to have been a safety feature as this would give a flat surface for the feet of shed staff when working on any of the pipe work in front of the cab. This plate had a number of vertical support struts. Locomotives known to have been fitted include Nos. 92000, 92001, 92002, 92206, 92211, 92219, 92220, 92233, 92240 and 92244. The preserved locomotives Nos. 92212, 92219 and 92220 still have this fitment.

Above: No. 92217 with a Tyseley (2a) shed code painted on the smoke box door. The locomotive has a flat plate over the reverser shaft as fitted to some WR-allocated locomotives. (IA)

Left: No. 92002 at Newport (Ebbw Junct) sometime before 1963 (when the shed code changed). The locomotive is fitted with a flat plate over the reverser shaft. In true 9F fashion the ash pan doors are open). (IA/JD)

CHAPTER SIX

PRESERVATION

Nine members of the class have been preserved
and five have been restored to operating condition.

A total of nine members of the 9F class have been preserved and a high proportion of these have been restored to traffic. Strangely only one of the locomotives, No. 92134, has a single chimney.

The locomotives preserved are as follows:

Number	Built	Location (as of December 2006)	Comments
No. 92134	Crewe 1957	Crewe Heritage Centre	The only single-chimney example, currently being restored at the Crewe Heritage Centre.
No. 92203	Swindon 1959	Gloucestershire & Warwickshire Railway	Withdrawn from BR and straight into preservation by the artist David Shepherd. No. 92203 travelled around the country on the mainline and on a number of preserved railways. Carries the name *Black Prince* on the smoke deflectors (last overhauled in 2000).
No. 92207	Swindon 1959	Shillingstone Station Project	Under restoration.
No. 92212	Swindon 1959	Mid Hants Railway	Awaiting boiler overhaul, restored at the Great Central Railway.
No. 92214	Swindon 1959	East Lancashire Railway	In full working order, normally based at the Midland Railway Centre.
No. 92219	Swindon 1960	Midland Railway Centre	Unrestored, in ex-Barry condition and there are no current plans to rebuild the locomotive.
No. 92220	Swindon 1960	National Railway Museum, York.	Has operated on the mainline since being preserved but is no longer operational.
No. 92240	Crewe 1958	Bluebell Railway	Restored to working order in 1990, now awaiting boiler repairs.
No. 92245	Crewe 1958	Barry Island, South Wales	Awaiting restoration.

The two injectors under the fireman's side of the cab. The Western Region route indicator (blue spot) is below the number and a single '9' is above the number. When the photograph was taken it was below freezing, hence the coal brazier in the foreground which was much appreciated by the author! (AC)

Right: No. 92203 on November 1967 on the last steam-hauled iron ore train from Bidston Docks (nr Birkenhead) to John Summers steel works at Shotton (on the Wirral) with the Chairman Sir Richard Summers seen in the cab. The locomotive was withdrawn from Birkenhead shed one week later and went straight into preservation having been purchased by the artist David Sheppherd. The buffers and other items at the front of No. 92203 have been painted white for the occasion. (IA)

The locomotives that have been restored are frequent visitors at many of the preserved railway lines, usually staying for a few months before moving on, so the list above only relates to the date it was created in January 2007.

CONCLUSION

The 9F was universally liked by the crews who operated the class. The locomotives were capable

of prodigious feats of haulage, both on heavy freight trains and express passenger trains.

Remarkably the whole class was only operational for four years (1960 to 1964) as the first withdrawal came in 1964 and of course the last locomotive built only entered service in 1960. The class had few problems to trouble the shed staff and the crews liked the free-steaming, sure-footedness and the ability of the locomotive to run smoothly at high speed. The class earned the nickname of

'spaceships' due to the height of the cab above the rails and the space between boiler and the frames. The author well remembers a conversation with some crews at 21A Saltley (Birmingham) depot in 1965 who remarked that they were the best steam locomotives they had ever worked.

The 9Fs were also liked by the staff of operating departments as they could schedule freight trains to run on heavily congested routes knowing that the locomotive could run at good speed and not get in the way of the passenger trains. It was also possible to complete a round trip in a day, rather than spending half of the time sat in a freight loop.

It is generally accepted that the 9F was the most successful of the BR 'Standard' classes and could be considered as one of the best classes of locomotive to have ever run on the BR network. The 9F was (and still is) an impressive looking locomotive.

Right: No. 92214 soon after restoration and showing the WR route indicator 'spot' in blue below the number. The flat plate fitted over the top of the reverser shaft was only fitted to a small number of WR-allocated locomotives. (AC)

Right: No. 92214 at Barrow Hill fitted with a BR1G tender, the type fitted to 9Fs on the Western Region. (AC)

Above: No. 92214 undergoing steam tests following restoration. The locomotive has a steam-heater pipe fitted to the front buffer beam (to the right of the coupling). (AC)

Left: No. 92203 on the ash pits at Loughborough. Note the Western Region route indicator (a blue spot below the number). The locomotive was initially allocated to the WR being shedded at Bristol, Old Oak Common and Banbury before going to the LM Region at Birkenhead in September 1966. (AC)

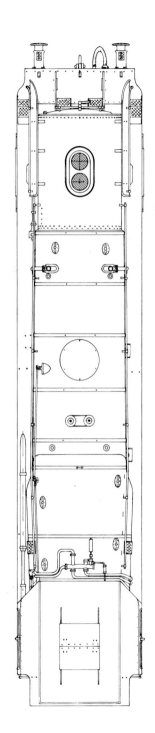

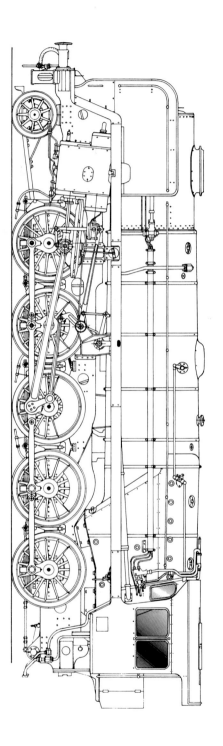

Riddles class 9F 2-10-0

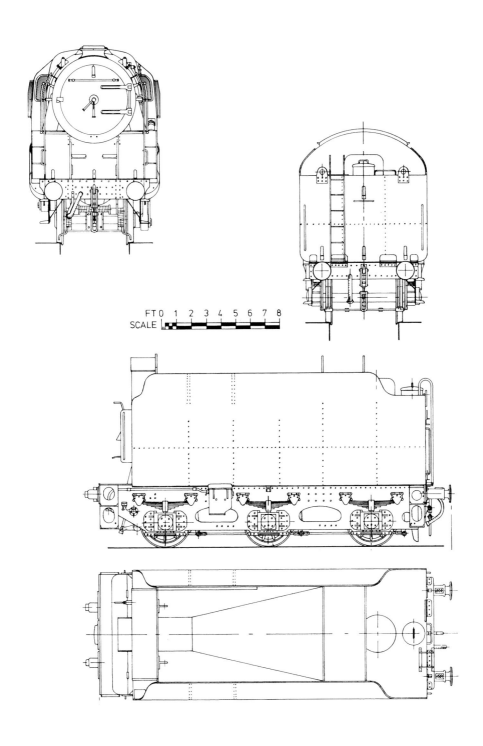

FT 0 1 2 3 4 5 6 7 8
SCALE

Standard BR1B tender

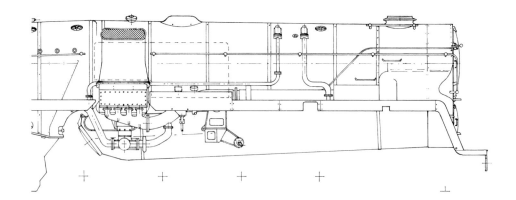

Riddles class 9F 2-10-0, Crosti boiler

© Copyright 2007 *Railway Modeller*/Ian Beattie

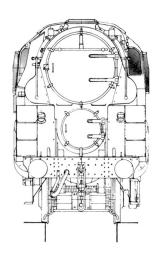

Below: No. 92024 a Crosti-boilered locomotive at Crewe works. Additional handrails are on the side and top of the smokebox to allow the fire raiser to close the lighting up chimney. (IA)

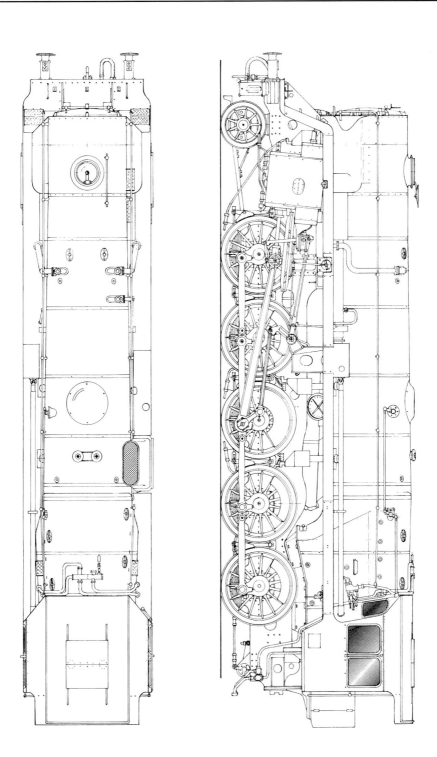

Riddles class 9F 2-10-0, Crosti boiler

Above: No. 92011 at Colwick (Nottingham) in 1966 when allocated to Birkenhead shed. The locomotive is fitted with the original BR1F tender. (AC)